Thank you to the generous team who gave their time and talents to make this book possible:

Author
Ellenore Angelidis and Leyla Angelidis

Illustrator
Daniel Aklilu

Creative directors
Caroline Kurtz, Jane Kurtz, and Kenny Rasmussen

Editors
Mastewal Abera and Woubeshet Ayenew

Designer
Beth Crow

Translator
Ahmed Dedo Gemeda

Ready Set Go Books, an Open Hearts Big Dreams Project

Mothers and Daughters: A Special Bond

Haadhoolii fi Ijoollee Dubaraa isaanii

English and Afaan Oromo

Mothers and daughters do lots of things together. This mom makes wonderful injera. Her daughter uses the leftovers to make fir fir.

Haati fi intalti isaanii wantoota hedduu waliin hojjeetu. Haati buddeena ajaa'ibaa tolchiti.Intalli ammoo firfirii buddeenaa hojjetti.

This mom grows vegetables for the family to eat. Her daughter loves looking at flowers nearby.

Haati kun maatii isheef kuduraalee man-duubatti biqilchiti. Intalli ishee ammoo abaaboowwan naannoo ishee jiran ilaaluu jaalati.

This mother shows her
daughter how to spin, just
the way she learned from
her own mother.

Haati akkaataa foo'aan
foo'amu haadha isheerraa
barattee intala ishee barsiifti.

Some mothers and daughters share stories. Her daughter likes to make her mom laugh.

Haadholiin tokko tokko intala isaanii waliin seenaalee dubbatu. Intalli kun harmee ishee kolfisiisu jaalatti.

This mom teaches her
daughter to braid hair.

Haati intala ishee rifeensa
dhahuu barsiifti.

This mom has always loved birds.
Her daughter is learning how to
protect them so they will be around
for future generations to enjoy.

aati kun simbirroota jaalatti. Intallis
akkamitti simbirroota eegdee
dhaloota dhufuuf tursuu akka
dandeessu barachaa jirti.

Mothers and daughters walk together to visit friends. They watch carefully for rocks.

Haati fi intalli hiriyyoota isaanii gaafachuuf waliin deemu. Gufuun akka isaan hindhoofne of-eeggannoodhaan tarkaanfatu.

This mom likes to look at the moon but
her daughter searches for shooting stars.

Haati kun ji'a ilaaluu jaalatti.
Intalli ishee garuu urjiilee
darbataman barbaaduu jaalatti.

Some mothers and daughters care for bees together. The daughter likes to chew on a bit of sweet beeswax.

Haadhooliifi ijoolleen durbaa tokko tokko kannisoota kunuunsu. Intalli jiisaa kannisaa mi'aawaa kuttee alanfachuu jaalatti.

Daughters and moms love to dance together. This daughter looks forward to when she can dance as well as her mom.

Intalli fi haati waliin shubbisuu jaalatu. Intalli kun akkuma harmee ishee hanga shubbisa sirriitti dandeessu dharraatetti.

Mothers and daughters like to play games together. This daughter loves to find special stones for the games.

Haadhaafi intalli waliin taphachuu jaalatu. Intalli, cirrachoota babbareedoo taphaaf ta'an funaanuu jaalatti.

Mothers and daughters all look for
chances to give each other big hugs
and say, "I love you!"

Haadhooliinifi ijoolleen dubaraa
hunduu wal-hammachuufi si jaaladha
waliin jechuuf carraawwan barbaadu.

About the Story

This book was written by the mother daughter team of Ellenore and Leyla Angelidis. They enjoy writing together and learning more about Leyla's amazing birth country. Ethiopia is home to many diverse cultures and geographies. Many more people live in the countryside than live in towns or cities. What mothers and daughters do together can vary greatly depending on where in Ethiopia they live. They might dance or share a laugh. A mother might spend quite a bit of time carrying her young daughter on her back, fixing her daughter's hair or teaching her daughter to cook. Mothers and daughters might work together for their families, feeding camels, grinding grain by hand, or carrying water long distances.

It is still the case in Ethiopia that women tend to have less education than men do and girls tend to have fewer educational opportunities than boys do—especially at the secondary level. But both government organizations and NGOs in Ethiopia are working to change that, including gender clubs in some schools. Research has shown that educating women means her children will become educated as well. Those women are able to contribute economically and work towards a better future for themselves, their families, and their communities.

Ethiopia currently has a number of mothers and daughters who are examples of leadership in Ethiopia and across Africa and the rest of the globe. Betelhem Dessie was just nine years old when she used her love of math and physics in the family shop. She has been named "the youngest pioneer in Ethiopia's fast emerging tech scene." For Frehiwot Tamru, CEO at Ethio telecom, it was a grandmother who taught her "about working toward your goal with a full heart." Some influential mothers are Sahle-Work Zewde, the first female head of state in Ethiopia's modern history, Meaza Ashenafi, the first female president of the supreme court, Aisha Mohammed Mussa, an engineer who currently serves as Minister of Irrigation and Lowland Areas Development and first female Defense Minister; and Bethlehem Tilahun Alemu, CEO of a successful footwear company.

About the Authors

Ellenore Angelidis is a public speaker, consultant, volunteer, lawyer, and aspiring writer. She stays busy with husband Michael and their three kids: two sons, Dimitri, Damian (who is an Open Hearts Big Dreams Junior Board member), and daughter, Leyla. Equalizing educational opportunities for children in Ethiopia is a passion that comes in part from being raised by two teacher parents and in part from raising an Ethiopian daughter. She founded and runs both OHBD and a new company L.E.A.D. (Lead Empower Activate Dream) LLC.

Leyla Marie Fasika Angelidis was born in Bahir Dar, Ethiopia and joined the Angelidis family in Seattle as an infant. She is currently in middle school and finds it unimaginable that some kids in her birth country don't get the chance to learn to read or go to school.

She has collaborated with her family to build a library in her birth town of Bahir Dar and to support other literacy projects through Open Hearts Big Dreams. She is an avid reader and aspiring writer. She has co-authored a number of OHBD Ready Set Go early reader books based on family experiences and personal interests. More recently, she is a featured spokesperson as well as helps with events and awareness building for OHBD literacy projects. Through these efforts she has learned more about her first country, language, and culture as well as positively contributed to her community in Ethiopia and in the US.

She has BIG DREAMS for herself and for kids living in Ethiopia (and around the world).

About the Illustrator

Daniel is from the capital city of Addis Ababa located in Ethiopia. He studied and graduated in BFA in Sculpture and MA in Fine Arts at Addis Ababa university, Alle School of Fine Arts and Design.

While working towards his post graduate degrees in Fine Arts he discovered his signature style. Through what he perceives as the disorders, crowds, and gaps in living standards within society Daniel has found a closeness between each area that we share that he looks to capture in his works. Highlighting what may be considered as a miscommunication between humanity in areas like language, culture and religion Daniel identifies the cause for barriers and conflict, which in some cases lead to greater consequences like violence and war.

In his own words: "Art and artists like myself represent a few among many in the world that can overcome differences, mostly because we use something that each of us share – the sense of sight. Whether through a painting, sculpture, photography, or illustration, anyone can form an opinion or engage with an artwork based on its appearance. I believe this sentiment is a perfect example of how we may see the same thing but appreciate it in different ways with no right or wrong conclusion. For this reason, this is what attracted me to art and design in the first place. As an artist, through my works I look to reshape the paradigm from what's "right and wrong" to what's "right and right.""

Starting from 2013 until today, Daniel is a full-time artist and professor at the Alle School of Fine Arts and Design at Addis Ababa University. The Alle School has played a pivotal role in Ethiopia and in Eastern Africa in general. It has been one of the most revered institutions of higher education where talented students have trained in pursuit of becoming professional artists and educators. As a professional artist himself, Daniel looks to help students understand art's historic impact, study standards of artistic expression, and develop and nurture a business acumen for those who look to add a commerce component to their portfolios.

About Open Hearts Big Dreams

Open Hearts Big Dreams Fund (OHBD) was founded by Ellenore Angelidis, inspired by her Ethiopian born daughter, Leyla Marie Fasika; both are key volunteers. OHBD is a United State 501(c)(3) not-for-profit organization that believes the chance to dream big dreams should not depend on where in the world you are born. Our mission is "Inspiring and empowering youth (K-14) to reimagine their futures by providing literacy, STEAM, and leadership opportunities."

OHBD harnesses the power of collaboration. We are made up of a small number of part-time paid staff and a large number of highly motivated volunteers with advanced skills, including artistic, editorial, translation, and high-tech expertise in Ethiopia, the Diaspora and globally. Our culture of innovation means we act fast on new ideas. Since 2017, we've produced more than 700 bilingual, culturally appropriate early reader titles and a number of STEM and Model programs to increase literacy, inclusion, and leadership.

In Ethiopia, for Ethiopia; OHBD is based in the U.S. but we are committed to working with local content creators and to producing quality books in Ethiopia. Local opportunities and production builds local knowledge and capacity.

About OHBD Ready Set Go Books

Reading has the power to change lives, but many children and adults in Ethiopia cannot read. One reason is that Ethiopia doesn't have enough books in local languages to give people a chance to practice reading. Ready Set Go books wants to close that gap and open a world of ideas and possibilities for kids and their communities.

When you buy an OHBD-RSG book, you provide critical funding to create and distribute more books.

Learn more at: http://openheartsbigdreams.org/book-project/ or find all our books at: https://ohbd-rsgbooks.com

OHBD Proudly Prints in Ethiopia

OHBD developed our own local printing capacity and have a number of our books available to pick up in Addis. They are available for bulk purchase and we regularly donate to schools, libraries and local organizations serving kids. Please contact us at ellenore@openheartsbigdreams.org if interested in samples or ordering.

So far, we have printed and distributed (with collaborating organizations) hundreds of thousands of copies of our books in numerous languages in country.

Our goal is to get these books to all elementary students across Ethiopia.

About Michael Carr's Legacy Project

Disability does not define a life. Mike Carr clearly demonstrated that his life was not defined by his disability. Although Mike was paralyzed at a young age, he still enjoyed a successful career with a high tech company in Seattle where both his technical skills and leadership were highly valued. Mike was a role model to so many of those he worked with and those who came to know him. He was a strong advocate for the power of inclusion and equal opportunity for individuals with disabilities. The legacy project in his name was created to provide opportunities for children with disabilities in Ethiopia, the birth country of one of his sons. Children with disabilities there do not lack talent or drive. What they too often lack, however, are the tools needed to develop these talents and to apply that drive.

Education remains the key to providing those tools. Unfortunately, educational opportunities for children with disabilities in Ethiopia are rare or in some cases, non-existent. The goal of the legacy project is to increase awareness of the educational disparities of Ethiopian children with disabilities and to increase educational opportunities for these children so they can become the role models of the future that Mike Carr was during his lifetime. Getting to see themselves in our Ready Set Go books is an important step to making this possible.

About the Language

The continent of Africa is home to many people who speak Afaan Oromo. Native speakers of Afaan Oromo, in fact, outnumber speakers of every other language except Arabic, Swahili and Hausa. Most Afaan Oromo speakers live in Ethiopia. (Many also live in the United States.) Using the Latin alphabet for writing Afaan Oromo can be traced back to the nineteenth century but was formally adopted in 1991.

About the Translation

Ahmed Dedo Gemeda is an Assistant Professor of English Language and Literature at Haramaya University. He is currently teaching undergraduate and postgraduate students. He is also serving as a translator, editor and reviewer on academic, technical and literary works.

Over 100+ unique OHBD-RSG books available in nearly 20 languages!

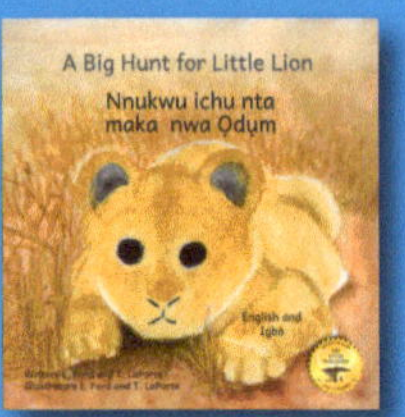 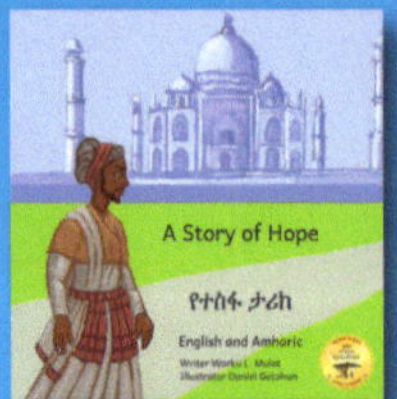 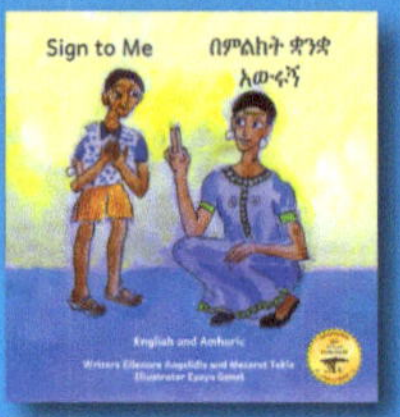  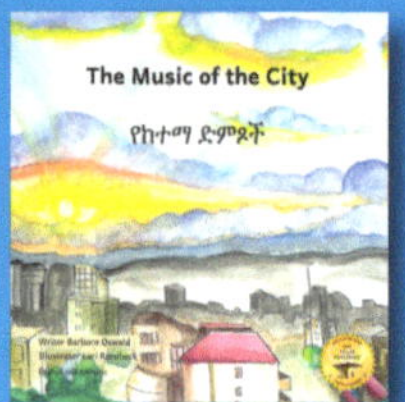 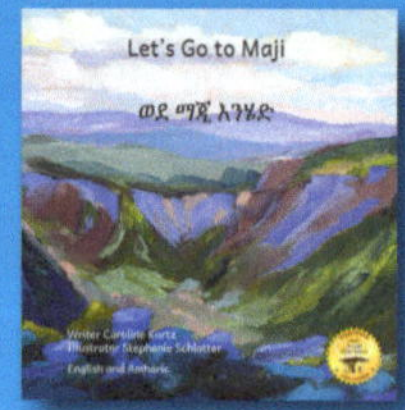

 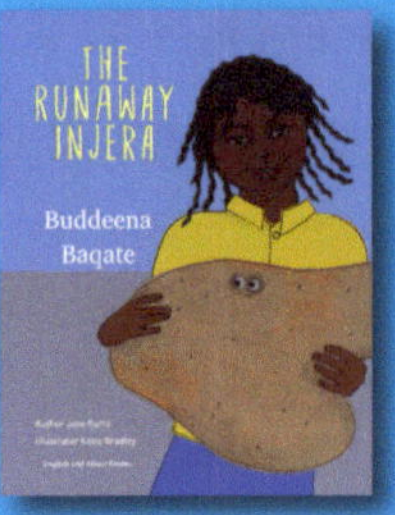  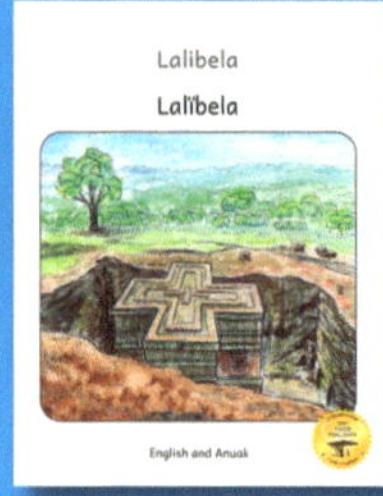 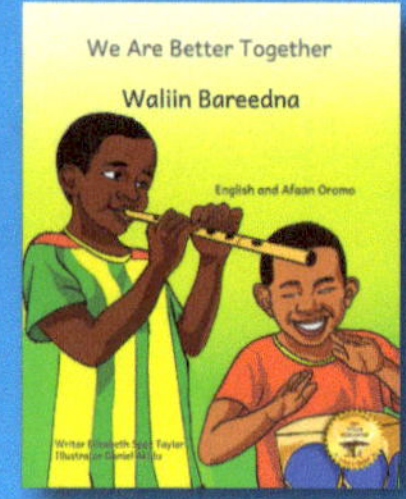 

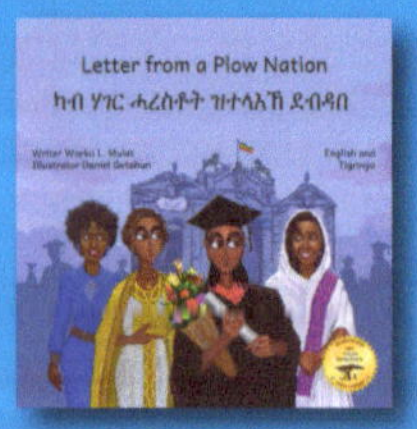 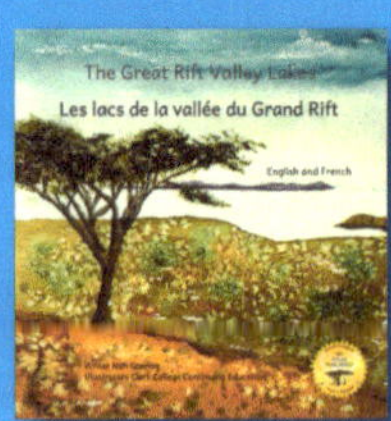 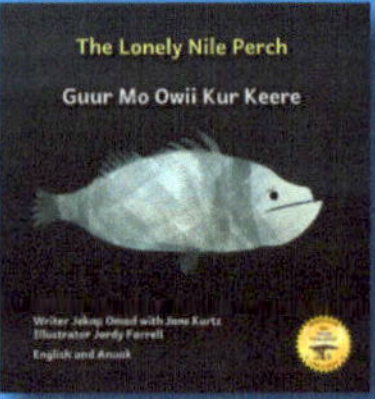 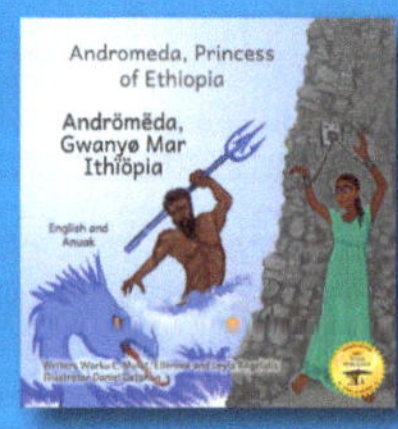 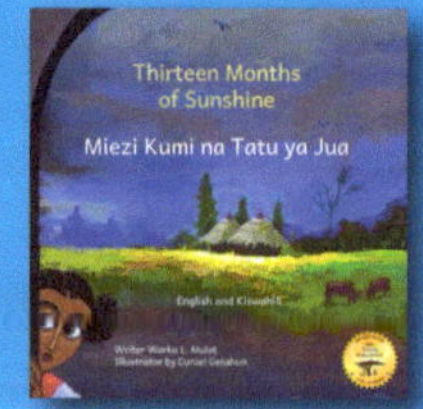 

To view all available titles, go to https://ohbd-rsgbooks.com/shop or scan QR code

Open Heart Big Dreams is pleased to offer discounts for bulk orders, educators and organizations.

Contact ellenore@openheartsbigdreams.org for more information.